JUST A MINUTE, LORD

YOUNG READERS

JUST A MINUTE, LORD

Prayers for Girls

LOIS WALFRID JOHNSON

AUGSBURG Publishing House • Minneapolis

TO ROY, GAIL, JEFFREY, AND KEVIN

JUST A MINUTE, LORD

Designed and illustrated by David Koechel.

Contents

I'm Looking Around, Lord

I'm Looking up, Lord

Preface

Do you know that you are a very special person?
A person so special
that God sent his Son, Jesus Christ,
to die for you?
Because of Jesus' death, your sins are forgiven.
With forgiveness, God also gives you his love:

Love which understands your bubbling fun times
and your everyday problems.
Love which accepts you just the way you are.
Love which gives you power to help you in your
daily life.

So curl up in your favorite corner
or look out the window into God's world.
Feel that you can say
whatever you like to him.
After you've used this book for awhile,
you might think of other things
you want to pray about.
Perhaps you'll discover your own way of saying,
"Just a minute, Lord."

7

I'm
Looking in,
Lord

Just a Minute, Lord

Lord,
you know that often I'm busy,
that I'm not good about sitting down
and saying long prayers.
Yet I need to talk to you.
I need to talk off and on
during the day,
the night.
I need to tell you things
I can't say to anyone else.
It's great to know
that even if I get rushed,
you're never too busy,
that you're always with me
ready to listen
when I want to pray
for just a minute.

Within the Stillness

Thank you for this quiet time
when the moments drop away
into forever,
plopping like spatters of rain
upon a window pane.
Thank you
that here within the stillness
I can think.
I can try to understand
the changes inside me—
in my feelings
in my thoughts
in my beliefs.
Thank you, Lord,
that you have found me here
and filled the empty space
of my heart.

I'm Afraid I'll Fail

I'm afraid I'll fail, Lord.
I'm trying,
but it isn't enough.
I'd like to please my parents.
I'd like to be
a big, round sugar cookie
perfectly made.
Yet when I'm scared of doing things,
I feel pushed
and ready to crumble
apart.
Please help my parents understand
that I can do some things well,
but there are other things
I'm not able to do.
And guide me, Lord,
so that I do my best
with the gifts
you have given me.

I Can't Feel Your Love

Lord,
sometimes I feel
the phone's gone dead.
I want to believe that you are there,
but I can't feel your love,
your strength,
and I keep wondering if the line is down.
Help me
when the going is rough
and I can't feel your nearness
to know that you love me,
and that
there's always a good connection
between
you and me.

It's Great To Be Alive!

It's great to be alive, Lord!
Some days have a special shine
as though
everything I do
is right.
Thank you for those times
when my friends are nice,
when school is going fine,
when a party is fun.
Thank you
for making me feel happy
all the way through.

I Don't Understand Myself

Lord,
when I'm angry
and full of hate
I don't understand myself.
One minute I'm happy,
and the next
I feel like a pop bottle
ready to fizz over.
Help me know
when I need
to uncap my feelings,
to let them out
by talking to someone else.
Lead me to people
who can help me.
Show me, too,
when there are times
I need to learn
to control my anger.

I Don't Like to Practice

I don't like to practice, God,
whether it's the piano,
or sewing,
or anything else.
Yet help me
when I'm tired
of trying to learn.
Remind me
that someday
I'll be glad
to know
the things
I've learned
today.

It's Fun to Play

Lord, it's fun
to run,
laugh,
shout.
To play
softball,
basketball,
volleyball.
To swim,
skate,
bike.
I feel
good all over
when I can play hard
and breathe in
great gulps of fresh air.
Thank, you, Lord,
for giving me a healthy body
so I can enjoy sports.

We're Moving, Lord

My parents say we're moving, Lord,
and in a way I look forward to it.
I know there'll be new things
to see and do.
Yet I get a funny feeling inside
when I think of leaving my friends.
I wonder
if I'll like my new school
and if my class will like me.
Remind me, Lord,
that I'm not really losing
everyone I know,
that instead
I'll be gaining new friends.
Remind me too
that you are my best friend
and will go with me
wherever I move.

Everything Has Gone Wrong

I feel terrible, Lord,
so terrible
that I want to crawl into bed,
pull up the covers,
and hide for awhile
with no one but you looking at me.
Why are some days so nice
and others horrible all the way?
Everything has gone wrong
since I got up this morning.
By now I feel
like taking it out
on someone else.
Be with me
when I feel hopeless and mean.
Remind me
that you always love me,
that even if I were a sparrow
with a broken wing,
you would notice
and care.

It's Hard to Wait

Lord,
it's so hard
for me
to wait.
The hours spin out into days
and the days seem week-long
when I'd like something special
to happen.
Be with me
when I want to leap ahead,
trying to force something
that isn't ready yet.
Help me understand
that you are the maker
of good things,
and that you will give them
to me
at the right time.

Why Are Clothes So Important?

Lord,
why do clothes become so important?
My mom complains
when she thinks I look sloppy.
She keeps telling me to dress nice
while I'm young
and have a good shape
to hang my clothes on.
Yet it means a lot to me
to do my own thing,
to look like the other girls.
Help both my mom and me
to understand
the way each other feels
so that clothes
don't come
between us.

I'm Lonely, Lord

I'm lonely, Lord.
I don't feel loved.
There's noise around me,
often there's a crowd.
I stand in the middle of the crowd
and I look around,
and I feel as though
I'm standing there
alone.
Isn't there a human being
who can take my loneliness away?
Someone who can reach out
and make me feel
that I belong?
I'm lonely, Lord.
I need your love.
I need the love
you gave when you died for me.
I need your love
because it's there forever.
Thank you, Lord!
Thank you.

I Feel Jumpy, God

Some days I feel jumpy, God.
I can't explain it even to myself.
It's as though there's a wondering
deep inside me,
a restlessness
that never quite gets answered.
Help me
when my restlessness
makes me do crazy things
or say words
I don't really mean.
Remind me
that I am held
in the palm
of your hand
and that your strong fingers
steady me,
offering me peace.

I Wish I Were Better Looking

God,
I wish I were better looking.
I'd like to have others notice me,
tell me I'm cute.
Yet I know that wishing
won't change the way I am.
Help me to do my best
with the face and body I have.
Make me beautiful inside
so that kindness and love
shine out
to those around me.

Thanks For Forgiveness

Lord, I'm sorry.
I'm sorry
for how selfish
I am.
I feel like that crumpled blouse
I threw on the floor
and kicked under my bed.
Thank you for promising
that you'll forgive me.
Wash me out.
Dry my tears.
Make me
fresh
and clean
again.

Lord, It's Exciting

Lord, it's exciting
when there's a new boy at school.
But some of the girls act silly
and spoil things.
I don't want
my friendships with boys
to be that way.
I want sex to be
like a white daisy
waving in the wind,
shining,
clean,
growing in bright sunlight.
Thank you, God,
that you have created me
with the ability
to give love.
Help me remember
that my body
is a special gift
made lovely
by you.

Make Me Well Soon

Lord,
I hate being sick
even if it's just the flu
or a bad cold.
I get panicky thinking
about what it must be like
being in bed
for weeks or months.
Give me the strength you had
when you suffered pain.
Remind me of the people you healed
while on earth.
If it is your will,
make me well soon.
Soon, Lord.
If you don't mind?

I Feel Like a Small Dot

God,
some days I feel like a small dot
in this huge universe.
I wonder why I am here.
Is there a reason for my birth?
I can't seem to see what it is,
yet you have given me talents,
gifts I can use
to work
for you.
Guide me
so that I see
how this tiny speck called me
can be a useful part of this world.
Show me your will
for my life.

Thanks For Music

Lord,
when I hear
the chirping
of a cardinal
or water rushing
over stones in a creek,
I think that you
must like music
the way I do.
Thanks for people
who give us music.
Thanks for the way
different moods of music
swell up within me
when I'm sad
or when I'm happy.
Thanks for words
that say things
I can't say myself.

I'm
Looking out,
Lord

Thanks For Encouragement

Lord,
you know better than anyone
how often I really try
to do good work
in school.
Sometimes, though,
I've wondered
if studying
is worth
all the effort.
Then you sent me a friend,
a teacher who wrote on my paper,
Super!
Great work!
Thank you, Lord,
for those words
I needed
to hear.

These Jobs Are Endless

Lord,
I get tired
of washing dishes
and cleaning my room.
It's just the same thing
over and over again.
Remind me
when I feel this way
that these jobs
are even more endless
for my mom.
Give me
a good feeling
when the dishes shine
or my room looks neat.
Help me learn
that daily tasks
aren't quite as bad
if I do them
quickly and well.

Help Me Be Honest, Lord

Help me be honest, Lord,
to accept the blame
if I've done something wrong.
Help me
when I'm tempted
to hide my mistake,
when I want to blurt out
that someone else did it.
Make me strong enough
to bury my pride,
and say,
"I'm sorry.
Will you forgive me?"

My Gift to You

Lord,
I'm like most girls I guess:
I'm pretty good at wasting
time and money,
and I've often heard
they're gifts
from you.
Help me
not to just know it
but also to feel it,
so that my use
of time and money
becomes
my gift
to you.

Thanks for Slumber Parties

Thank you
for slumber parties
where
we can
giggle together,
gobble popcorn and pizza,
play records,
and talk all night.
Thank you, Lord,
for friends
with whom
I can share good fun.

Getting Along with My Mom

God,
you know that now and then
I have a hard time
getting along with my mom.
Sometimes she doesn't understand me,
and I don't understand her either.
Yet today
she was really kind of nice,
not nagging,
just nice!
Thank you, God.

Thanks for Relatives

For aunts
and uncles,
grandmas,
grandpas,
special
cousins,
sisters,
brothers—
for all my relatives
who like to hear
what I'm doing,
who make me feel
as though
I'm somebody—
Thank you, Lord!

Thanks for Funny Things

Thank you for funny things,
for the bubbling feeling of giggles
that fill my insides,
push up,
and spill over
in a shout of joy!
Thank you, Lord.
Thank you!

Help Me Help Her

Mom's been working hard, Lord.
I can tell
because she's tired
and a little bit on edge.
Forgive me
for wanting to escape
and avoid any work I can.
Help me
to help her
so that
she doesn't feel
she has to do everything
by herself.

I Was Angry, God

I was angry, God,
and in that moment
the words spilled out,
words
that brought a hurt look
to my mom's eyes
and an angry flush
to my dad's face.
I'm sorry
for the things I said.
Will you forgive me?
Will you break up
the tightness around my heart
that keeps me from saying
I'm sorry
to them?

Thanks For Parents

Father,
Thank you for my parents:
for mom's warmth
and dad's strength,
for the way
they make me feel better
when I'm upset,
for the way they both know
what is going on,
even if it sometimes means
I can't have my own way.
Thank you
for the love they give me
when I act as though
I think they're square.
Thank you
that they love me enough
to correct me
when I do something wrong.
And thank you, God,
that I can tell you
how much my parents mean to me,
because I'm just not able
to tell them.

Thanks For Color, Lord

Lord,
you could have made everything
in black and white,
but it's so much
nicer this way.
Thank you for the colors
in my curtains and bedspread,
in my clothes and books.
Thank you
for the blues and whites
of the sky,
for the darkness
of earth
freshly plowed,
and the reds and yellows
of flowers
saying hello
to the sun.
Thank you
for every color
in the rainbow,
and for the eyes
you have given me
to see.

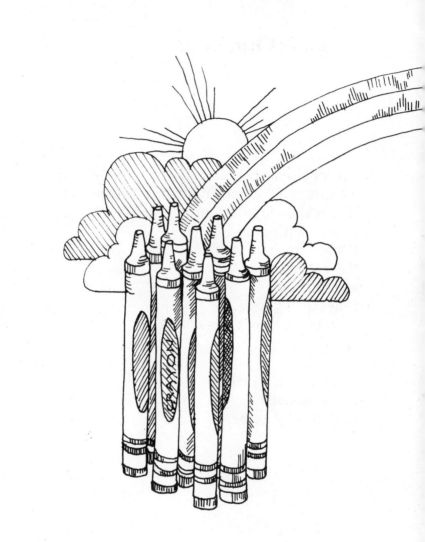

School's Out, Lord!

School's out, Lord!
The days of summer stretch before me
like waves lapping on a beach
bright with sun.
I want to run on that beach,
the soft sand
spitting out
beneath my toes.
I want to shout *freedom!*
freedom!
freedom!
Thank you, Lord,
for vacations
that finally come.

It Was Fun, God

It was fun, God—
seeing new places,
swimming,
fishing,
camping in the woods,
hearing small animals
call in the night,
falling asleep,
knowing that we were
all close together.
Thank you
for the warm times
our family shares
on vacation.

Marriage Seems Far Away

Getting married seems far away,
and yet
girls I know
are already thinking
about it.
Often the whole idea scares me,
and other times I think
it might not be so bad
after all.
Will you show me, Lord,
what things are important
for a good marriage?
Guide me
when I start to date
so that
I go with
the right kind
of boys.

My Little Brother

Lord,
I've talked to you quite often
about my little brother.
You know how mad I've been,
how I've cried about his teasing,
and how I've prayed that I could
somehow
love him?
Well, today I have to tell you
something great.
It's hard to believe,
but he seems changed.
(Not really nice yet
but improved.)
I don't know what happened,
but whatever it was,
thank you!

I'm
Looking Around,
Lord

I'm Worried about People

Lord,
I'm worried about people:
forgotten older people,
children without parents,
prisoners of war,
fathers without work,
people who have no homes,
who are hungry and cold,
or who live with problems
that wind them up tight
inside.
Show me how I can help
these other people.
Give me the right words
to tell them
of your love.

The Sky Grew Black

Yesterday the sky grew black
and the wind and rain
rattled the windows.
I was frightened, God.
But then I knew
that you're the only one
with the power
to create storms,
that this is your way
of sending water
to make crops grow
and give us food.
Thank you, God,
for caring
for us.

Help Me Unlabel Them

I look at people with labels—
those who are
too fat,
too tall,
too awkward,
or too homely.
I don't really want
to be friends with them, Lord.
I'd like to avoid them
if I could,
the way others do.
Yet I know you don't want me
acting that way,
for you treated the rich and the poor,
the popular and the unpopular,
just the same.
Help me
so that I no longer
label others.
Help me love everyone
the way you love
all of us.

How Can I Tell Her?

Lord,
you know my friend isn't a Christian
and it bothers me.
I feel as though I should tell her
about you
and your love.
But it scares me,
and I don't know where to start.
Help me, Lord,
to live in such a way
that she will want to know
about you.
Make me
like a tall glass
of cold milk,
filled
and running over
with your happiness.

What Is It Like to Die?

Jesus,
what is it like to die?
I know that sooner or later
everything dies—
cats,
dogs,
parakeets,
even people—
and that just as we are all born
we will also
all die.
Thank you for making death
something that can be happy,
that when I die
you will be with me,
that you will be standing
at the door of your home
to welcome me to heaven.
Thank you for rising
from the dead
and for going ahead
to prepare
a beautiful place
for me.

I'm Sure of You

Lord,
so many junior-high girls
try smoking now and then.
I know all about lung cancer,
but that seems far away
when others tell me
I'm a sissy
for not smoking.
Lord,
I don't want cigarettes
to be a security blanket
to hang onto
when I'm not sure
of myself.
Remind me
that I don't need any blanket,
that I can be sure of you
and of your power
to help me.

Let Me See Them as Persons

God our Father,
help me not to see people
as different races,
as red
or yellow,
black
or white.
Instead
let me see them
as persons
who feel,
who laugh,
who cry,
who hurt or hate or love
just as I do.

The Power to Say No

Lord,
I want to thank you
for all the medicines we have
that help cure diseases.
Yet there's an uneasiness inside me
that won't go away.
I hear about teenagers
who are turning on with drugs
and it bothers me, Lord.
I need you here.
Help me
if others ask me to try things.
Give me the strength to say no
and no
and no again.
Remind me
that I don't need something
to put me down
or build me up,
that the power
you have given me
helps me live
just the way
I am.

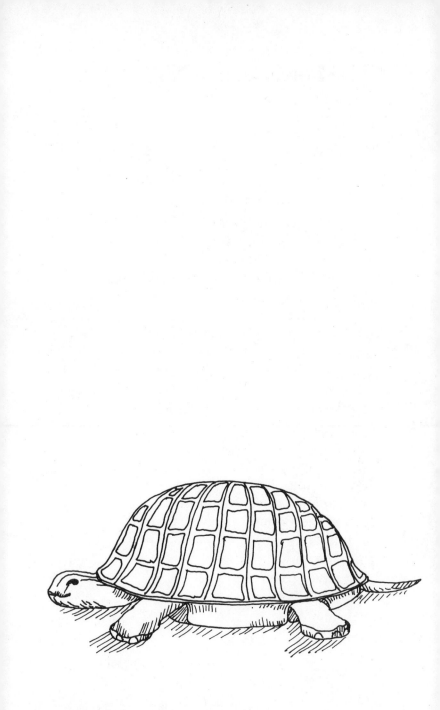

Choosing Friends

Lord,
I'm not sure
about some of my friends.
Often I feel
like a pet turtle
trying to climb the walls
of a slippery bowl
but unable
to get out.
Help me to love everyone
but also
to choose
as my special friends
those who will help me
live the right way.

When I Babysit

Lord,
often my mom asks me
to take care
of my younger brother or sister.
Sometimes it scares me.
I know how fast
they can get into something
or fall
and hurt themselves.
Be with me
whenever I baby-sit
so that I don't forget
my responsibility
to the children
I'm caring for.
Help me see the things
which are dangerous to them.
Help me
know what they need.
Show me
how to give them love.

I Want To Be In, Lord

I want to be in, Lord.
I want to be part of the crowd,
to have others accept me
for myself.
Yet why does being in
mean saying yes
to so many things?
I don't want to say yes
when it's wrong,
but I don't want
to be left out of things either.
You didn't give in to everybody.
You wanted to do
the will of your Father.
But didn't it bother you sometimes?
Wasn't it hard being alone?
Will you show me the answer, Lord?
Will you give me the power to say no?

I'm
Looking up,
Lord

Are You Smiling, Lord?

Lord,
Do you smile
just a bit
when I pray
my silly little prayers?
It's great to know
that I can say anything to you,
that there's nothing too small
for you.
Thank you
for answering my prayers,
for promising
to be with. me
always.

I Have So Many "Why's?"

God,
often there are things
I don't understand.
I have so many "why's?"
and I can't find the answers.
Help me believe
in you
even when
I don't understand everything
about you.
Create in me
the trust
and the faith
which I need.

Make Me Feel like Popcorn

Lord,
sometimes it's boring
sitting in church.
I wonder why
it has no meaning for me.
Yet
other times
you seem so near,
and I know how much
you care.
Remind me, Lord,
when religious things
seem to drag,
that you're a living person
and you understand
when I'm wiggly
and find it hard
to sit still.
Make me feel
like popcorn
bursting into life
with the joy
of knowing you.

The Magic of a New Day

Thank you, Lord,
for the splash of color
you have used
to wash the darkness
from the sky.
Thank you
for the freshness
of the sun
brightening the earth,
for the magic
of a new day,
a new beginning.

Hold My Hand

God,
I don't believe
you're a stern old man
with a long beard
and a white robe.
I think of you
as a loving Father
who is kind
and wants to hold my hand
as you have
for children
throughout all time.
Thank you!

Speak To Me

Now and then
when I read the Bible
I feel as though
I'm left
in
the
dark.
I don't know how
it applies
to the everyday me.
Help me, Lord,
when I'm puzzled
and don't understand.
Turn on your flashlight,
brightening my mind and soul.
Speak to me
through your Word.

Both Strong and Gentle

How strong you are, God,
as strong as an ocean wave
dancing against
tall rocks.
Yet how gentle you are too,
as gentle
as pale moonlight
softening the darkness.
Thank you for being
both strong and gentle,
both mighty and kind.

Thanks for the Change of Seasons

Thank you, God,
for the change of seasons:
for the dry leaves
that whisper and crunch
as I walk,
for the ice ponds
ready for skating,
for the warm winds of spring
and the kites flying high,
for the call of summer
and the tall trees
dressed in new leaves.
Thank you, God,
for the wonder
found each time of year.
Thank you
that during this change
you do not change,
that you are always with me.

Keep Me from Wanting

God and Father,
it's hard for me to be thankful
because I've never known
what it's like
to still be hungry
after I've eaten,
or to wear clothes
with holes too big to mend.
Thank you
for all the things
I'm so used to having
that I forget others go without.
Thank you
for chocolate cakes and hamburgers,
for my own bed and a soft pillow,
for warm houses
with families in them.
Keep me from wanting
so many things
that I forget
how much
other people need.

It Was for Me!

Jesus,
sometimes your death
on the cross
seems far away.
Then I remember
that it wasn't
just for my mom,
and dad,
or my friends
that you died.
It was for
me,
me,
me!
And then
your suffering
and your forgiveness
are real.
Thank you
for taking my place.

You Are Alive!

So often I don't stop to think
about Easter's real meaning.
I need to jump out of bed,
run to the garden,
hear for myself
the angel saying,
"He has risen, he is not here!"
Surprise me, Lord!
Fill me with the joy
of that early morning,
so that I understand
what it means for me
that you are
alive!
alive!
alive!

Fill Me, Lord

Lord,
you know I can't see the wind blow.
Yet I can see leaves or dust
pushed by the wind.
And I wonder,
is that how the Holy Spirit works?
Giving power
to ordinary people like me?
Take my life, Lord.
Fill me
with the Spirit's power.
Make me willing
to allow you
to lead
me.

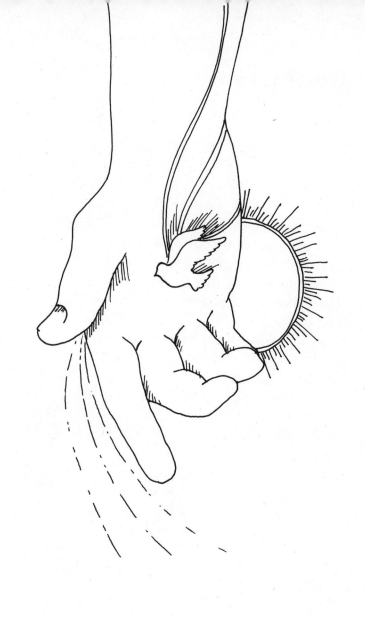

Bless Me Now

Lord,
bless me now
as I go out into your world.
Let me feel your love,
experience your forgiveness,
and sense your power
within me.
Give me your understanding
so that I can understand others.
Shower upon me
your hope,
your peace,
your joy.